Table of Contents

Introduction

The purpose of this book is to provide an honest and critical look at the New Testament. While the New Testament has grown to be the foundation of many religions and sects as well as a source of inspiration for many, it is laden with errors, contradictions and discrepancies. The same has been found with the history of Jesus as found within the New Testament. This book will serve as a critical analysis of the story of Jesus and the New Testament with the expectation of nothing more than spreading the truth. Readers are encouraged not to only read this book, but to study and research the topics discussed within this book, then reach their own conclusions.

The primary biblical translation that will be used within this text is the King James Version of the Holy Bible. This text will be used simply because it is the most popular and most readily available. Also, the terms Old Testament and New Testament will be used for communication purposes, as it relates to the Hebrew Scriptures and Greek Scriptures respectively, with the full realization that there is only one true testament of the Most High.

A Virgin Shall Bear a Son

One of the major pillars of the Christian faith is based on a prophecy that has been improperly represented as foretelling the birth of Jesus. Matthew 1 speaks of the genealogy of Jesus and Mary being pregnant by the Holy Spirit. Joseph seeks to end his engagement with Mary after realizing she is pregnant. It is then stated that Joseph was approached by an angel in a dream, and informed that he should not end his engagement with Mary, because she is impregnated by the Holy Spirit and will give birth to Jesus. It goes on to state in Matthew 1: 22-23 the following:

"(1:22) Now all this was done, that it might be fulfilled which was spoken of the Lord by the prophet, saying, (1:23) Behold, a virgin shall be with child, and shall bring forth a son, and they shall call his name Emmanuel, which being interpreted is, God with us."

The writer *(Matthew)* of this text is stating clearly that the whole purpose of the birth of Jesus was the fulfillment of a

3

previously stated prophecy. The prophecy of which he speaks of is found in Isaiah 7:14 and it states the following:

"(7:14) Therefore the Lord himself shall give you a sign; Behold, a virgin shall conceive, and bear a son, and shall call his name Immanuel"

Without further research it may appear to some as if the two prophecies match. However, we must now analyze the prophecy stated as being fulfilled by the birth of Jesus. First, let's establish a few facts:

(1) Isaiah was born approximately 765BCE and began prophesying 739BCE.[1] This is over 700 years before the birth of Jesus. (*This fact is accepted almost universally by historians and theologians of all faiths and denominations. These dates are easily determined by kings in power during his prophecies and can be easily confirmed.*)

---

[1] Richard's Complete Bible Dictionary, World Bible Publishers, Inc, 2002, p. 523 *(ISBN 0-529-11490-9)*

(2) Isaiah was prophesying to King Ahaz for a specific reason and Ahaz was intended to see the fulfillment of the prophecy. *(This fact will be proven through a review of the text) (See: Isaiah 7:10-11).*

A common unfortunate occurrence is that individuals sometimes read one biblical verse and take it out of context. In order to fully understand this prophecy one must read and understand the verses preceding and following the prophecy. The verses preceding the prophecy embraced by Matthew and Christianity are as follows:

Isaiah 7: 1-16

"(7:1) And it came to pass in the days of Ahaz the son of Jotham, the son of Uzziah, king of Judah, that Rezin the king of Syria, and Pekah the son of Remaliah, king of Israel, went up toward Jerusalem to war against it, but could not prevail against it. (7:2) And it was told the house of David, saying, Syria is confederate with Ephraim. And his heart was moved, and the heart of his people, as the trees of the wood are moved with the wind. (7:3) Then said the LORD unto Isaiah, Go forth now to meet Ahaz, thou, and Shearjashub thy son, at

5

the end of the conduit of the upper pool in the highway of the fuller's field; (7:4) And say unto him, Take heed, and be quiet; fear not, neither be fainthearted for the two tails of these smoking firebrands, for the fierce anger of Rezin with Syria, and of the son of Remaliah. (7:5) Because Syria, Ephraim, and the son of Remaliah, have taken evil counsel against thee, saying, (7:6) Let us go up against Judah, and vex it, and let us make a breach therein for us, and set a king in the midst of it, even the son of Tabeal: (7:7) Thus saith the Lord GOD, It shall not stand, neither shall it come to pass. (7:8) For the head of Syria is Damascus, and the head of Damascus is Rezin; and within threescore and five years shall Ephraim be broken, that it be not a people. (7:9) And the head of Ephraim is Samaria, and the head of Samaria is Remaliah's son. If ye will not believe, surely ye shall not be established. (7:10) Moreover the LORD spake again unto Ahaz, saying, (7:11) Ask thee a sign of the LORD thy God; ask it either in the depth, or in the height above. (7:12) But Ahaz said, I will not ask, neither will I tempt the LORD. (7:13) And he said, Hear ye now, O house of David; Is it a small thing for you to weary men, but will ye weary my God also? (7:14) Therefore the Lord himself shall give you a sign; Behold, a virgin shall conceive, and

6

bear a son, and shall call his name Immanuel. (7:15) Butter and honey shall he eat, that he may know to refuse the evil, and choose the good. (7:16) For before the child shall know to refuse the evil, and choose the good, the land that thou abhorrest shall be forsaken of both her kings."

If that seemed confusing, here is a synopsis of the events surrounding this prophecy. Ahaz was the king of Judah at the time. Pekah *(the king of Israel)* and Rezin *(the king of Syria)* joined together to fight against Ahaz and his kingdom. The prophet Isaiah and his son Shearjashub were sent by the Lord to prophesy to King Ahaz. Isaiah's prophecy was to inform Ahaz not to worry about the two invading armies. After the prophecy Ahaz was asked to request a sign from the Lord, but he refused *(See: Isaiah 7:10-12)*. Therefore, the Lord informed him of a sign to come that will validate the prophecy. The sign that was given is that *"Behold, a virgin shall conceive, and bear a son, and shall call his name Immanuel."* This is the prophecy at the center of the virgin birth theory of Christianity.

There are many reasons why Matthew's misinterpretation of this prophecy as the foretelling of Jesus is both impossible and incorrect. First, it is clearly established that the *"virgin birth"* of a child was intended as a sign for King Ahaz to see. The intent of the sign is to prove that he didn't have to worry about the two invading armies. Secondly, this prophecy occurred over 700 years prior to the birth of Jesus. King Ahaz did not live 700 hundred years beyond this point. In fact he died at the age of 36.[2] This clearly demonstrates that Ahaz never saw the birth of Jesus; therefore, the prophecy could not have been talking about Jesus. It is simply mathematically impossible, due to the timelines, for this prophecy to be in reference to Jesus.

This leaves us with an interesting dilemma. According to Matthew in the first chapter he stated that all of the events leading up to the birth of Jesus were in fulfillment of a prophecy of the Lord. Matthew 1:22-23 states: *"(1:22) Now all this was done, that it might be fulfilled which was spoken of the Lord by the prophet, saying,*

---

[2] (2 Kings 16:2) and (2 Chronicles 28:1) states that Ahaz was twenty years old when he began to reign and reigned only sixteen years.

(1:23) Behold, a virgin shall be with child, and shall bring forth a son, and they shall call his name Emmanuel, which being interpreted is, God with us." This is clearly impossible and untrue. Also, nowhere in the entire New Testament was Jesus ever called Emmanuel; they called him Jesus. In fact, the name Emmanuel is not written anywhere else in the entire New Testament besides this verse. There is a falsehood in the first chapter of the first book of the New Testament *(Matthew Chapter 1);* how can the validity of the text be established? Also, if Matthews's belief system was entirely based on the misunderstanding of a prophecy, then his entire belief system may very well be incorrect.

Other Observations Regarding the "Virgin Birth"

Many scholars now admit that the Hebrew word translated as *virgin*, in this verse *(Isaiah 7:14)*, does not mean virgin in Biblical Hebrew. The Hebrew word that was translated as virgin is pronounced *al-mah*. Al-mah simply means a young woman. The word used to mean a virgin in Biblical Hebrew is pronounced *bet-oo-la.*[3]. This fact is recognized in translation of many of the new

---

[3] The following verses correctly demonstrate that the Biblical Hebrew word for

Christian Bibles, such as the Revised Standard Version of the Holy

Bible.

The Resurrection

Another item at the core of the Christian faith is that of the resurrection. Jesus is said to have risen from the dead after being crucified. The resurrection is discussed within the New Testament several times by several authors all giving varying accounts of the circumstances surrounding the resurrection. It is absolutely essential to the Christian faith for the resurrection of Jesus to be true. Paul acknowledges this fact in (1 Corinthians 15: 14-15). Which states, *"(15:14) And if Christ be not risen, then is our preaching vain, and your faith is also vain. (15:15) Yea, and we are found false witnesses of God; because we have testified of God that he raised up Christ: whom he raised not up, if so be that the dead rise not"*

Paul's comments state simply that if Jesus did not rise from the dead then the Christian faith is in vain. Multiple and varying accounts are given on the resurrection of Jesus. The main texts on the resurrection are found in the following scriptures: Matthew 28, Mark 16, Luke 24 and John 20-21. Each telling of the course of events surrounding the resurrection varies. Reading each of these

11

varying accounts will uncover multiple discrepancies in the resurrection story. These four versions of the resurrection story clearly contradict each other in many different ways. Let's review the most glaring contradictions.

Who were the people that came to the tomb and how many people came?

1) According to Matthew (28:1) two people came, Mary Magdalene and the other Mary.

2) Mark (16:1) states that three people came: Mary Magdalene, Mary the Mother of James and Salome.

3) Luke (24:10) declares that more than four people came to the tomb. Mary Magdalene, Mary the mother of James, Joanna and other woman.

4) According to John (20:1) only Magdalene came to the tomb.

When the people came to the tomb was the sun up?

1) Mathew (28:1) says it was dawn and Luke (24:1) says it was early in the morning

2) Mark (16:2) says that they came to the tomb at sun rise

3) John (20:1) states that Mary came to the tomb while it was yet dark

Was there an angel at the tomb or a young man? What was he/they doing?

1) Matthew says that it was one angel sitting on the stone that he rolled away from the tomb (28:2).

2) Mark says that it was one young man sitting on the right side inside the tomb (16:5)

3) Luke says there were two men standing by them inside the tomb.

4) According to John when Mary first arrives to the tomb there are no angels present. When Mary returns she finds two angels, one sitting by the head and one at the feet. (20:1-2,12)

Who carried the cross?

1) Mathew (27:32), Mark (15:21), Luke (23:26) all state that Simon of Cyrene carried the cross.

2) While John insists that Jesus himself carried the cross (John19:17).

What time was it when Jesus was crucified?

1) Mark (15:25) says that it was the third hour when they crucified him

2) However, John (19:14-15) proclaims that Jesus was not crucified until after the sixth hour.

What were Jesus' last dying words on the cross?

1) According to Mathew (27:46) and Mark (15:34) it was Eli *(Eloi)*, Eli *(Eloi)* lama sabachthani? Meaning, "My God, my God why has thou forsaken me?"

2) Luke (23:46) states that his last words were, "Father into thy hand I commend my spirit"

3) John (19:30) says that Jesus merely said, "It is finished"

Did either of the two thieves being crucified with Jesus believe him?

1) Mathew (27:44) agrees with Mark (15:32) that neither one of the thieves believed in Jesus.

2) Luke (23:39-42) contradicts both accounts and states one of the thieves does not believe while the other one does.

When were the spices prepared?

1) Mark (16:1) declares that Mary prepared the spices after the Sabbath was over.

2) Luke (23:54-56) states that Mary prepared the spices before the Sabbath started.

3) John (19:39) contradicts both of the previous reports by stating that Nicodemus prepared the spices before the Sabbath.

Clearly by reviewing the text of the varying accounts one can continue to find additional contradictions. However, listing all of the contradictions of the resurrection story can be a book all of its own. My efforts were merely to demonstrate that the vast inconsistencies in the accounts of Jesus' resurrection are too numerous to overlook. Furthermore, it is not possible to determine what, if any, part of the story is true because it is not consistent. At the center of one of the most significant pillars of Christianity lie contradictions, discrepancies and falsehoods. If no resurrection has occurred than there is no grounds for Christianity. Remember as stated earlier Paul proclaims correctly in (1 Corinthians 15: 14-15) *"(15:14) And if Christ be not risen, then is our preaching vain, and your faith is also vain. (15:15) Yea, and we are found false witnesses of God; because we have testified of God that he raised up Christ: whom he raised not up, if so be that the dead rise not"*.

It is extremely difficult to reasonably believe whole-heartedly in the resurrection of Jesus after a careful review of its related text. According to Paul's statement this makes the Christian faith vain, along with its related preaching. Furthermore, one is considered a false witness of God if they proclaim God raised Jesus from the dead if he didn't raise him from the dead.

God's Only Begotten Son

The New Testament verse credited with being translated into the most languages is John (3:16). This verse has become the slogan of many preachers, pastors, reverends and ministers of many Christian denominations and believers of the New Testament doctrine. John (3:16) states: *"For God so loved the world, that he gave his **only begotten Son**, that whosoever believeth in him should not perish, but have everlasting life."* Without immediately addressing the fundamental and blatant injustice, of having an unrelated and unassociated individual suffer and crucified for the sin of others, I will discuss the falsehood of Jesus being God's *"Only Begotten Son"*.

The word "only" by definition refers to one person, place or thing. So according to John's rendition of history, Jesus was God's only son. Notice that John didn't state that Jesus was one of God's sons or even that he was the favorite of God's sons. He declared that he was God's only begotten son. This statement by John blatantly contradicts numerous biblical references. For example:

17

(Exodus 4:22) *states, "And thou shalt say unto Pharaoh, Thus saith the LORD, **__Israel is my son, even my firstborn__**"*. Many believers in the New Testament doctrine disregard this verse as a metaphor, though this verse states, *"Thus saith the Lord"*. This in essence implies that they believe John's word over the Lord's. One can argue that if the Lord said Israel is his son, even his firstborn son that he is correct. I am certain that no one of a righteous or logical mind would argue that the Lord doesn't know his son, especially his first born son.

Several other biblical verses that obviously contradicts John's claim that Jesus is God's only begotten son are found within the book of Genesis. There are several references within the book of Genesis that refer to the **Sons of God**. Of course, if God has Sons *(plural)* it would be impossible for Jesus to be God's only begotten son *(singular)* as stated by John. Verses in the book of Genesis that speak of the Sons of God are as follows:

18

(Genesis 6:2) *"That the **Sons of God** saw the daughters of men that they were fair; and they took them wives of all which they chose"*

(Genesis 6:4) *"There were giants in the earth in those days; and also after that, when the **Sons of God** came in unto the daughters of men, and they bare children to them, the same became mighty men which were of old, men of renown.*

The book of Genesis is not the only area with the biblical text that refers to God having multiple sons. References to the Sons of God are also found within the book of Job. While reviewing these verses, keep in mind that John stated that Jesus was God's only begotten son. Furthermore, the texts surrounding these references, as with the text in Genesis, indicate clearly that the Sons of God are heavenly beings. Therefore, it cannot be summarily passed over as merely a metaphor. The verses in the book of Job are as follows:

(Job 1:6) *"Now there was a day when the **Sons of God** came to present themselves before the LORD, and Satan came also among them."*

19

(Job 2:1) *"Again there was a day when the **Sons of God** came to present themselves before the LORD, and Satan came also among them to present himself before the LORD"*

Both previously stated references clearly indicate that there was a meeting with God, his Sons *(plural)* and Satan. This cannot be confused with earthly beings or metaphoric Sons of God because they were in the presence of God and Satan. Therefore, it must have been heavenly beings. Once again, this demonstrates that John's statement and belief, that Jesus was God's only begotten son is incorrect and contradictory to numerous biblical references.

One may correctly notice that the references stated as conflicting with John's statement in John (3:16) are all from the "Old Testament". Many of those not knowledgeable of the bible may utilize this fact to state that the "Old Testament" is no more or no longer relevant. However, such a statement ignores the fact that Malachi (3:6) states *"**For I am the LORD, I change not**; therefore ye sons of Jacob are not consumed."* If the Lord states that he does

20

not change, one can righteously and logically conclude that His comments and declarations also do not change.

Furthermore, if one believes in the New Testament and Jesus, then certain things should be evident. There was no "New Testament" during Jesus' time. Furthermore, Jesus is stated as believing in the law and prophets of the "Old Testament." In Matthew (5:17) Jesus is recorded as saying, *"Think not that I am come to destroy the law, or the prophets: I am not come to destroy, but to fulfill."* The only law or prophets of whom Jesus could have been speaking are those of the "Old Testament" because they are the only references that would have been available during that time period.

One common rationalization made by many defenders of the concept of Jesus being God's only begotten son, is to emphasize the word **begotten.** Their argument is that while there are many references to "Sons of God", Jesus is his ***only begotten son.*** However, this argument is inadequate. It becomes even more inadequate while considering Psalm (2:7). In Psalms (2:7) God refers to David as being his begotten son. Psalms (2:7) says, I will declare the decree: the Lord hath said unto me, ___thou art my son this day have I begotten thee___. This clearly states that according to God, David is his begotten son. If David is his begotten son, how can Jesus be his only begotten son?

Moreover, many New Testament verses contradict John's assertion that Jesus is God's only begotten son. Matthew (5:45, 48) states, "That ye may be children of your father" and "Be ye therefore perfect as your father which is in heaven is perfect". They are all referred to as God's children and God is referred to as their father. Adam is also called the Son of God in Luke (3:38). Moreover, Jesus is referred to as being the "Son of Man" several times throughout the "New Testament". For those that don't believe that Jesus is the "Son of a Man" maybe they will believe it if he said it. Fortunately, Jesus does refer to himself as the son of man:

(Matthew 16:13) *"When Jesus came into the coasts of Caesarea Philippi, he asked his disciples, saying, Whom do men say that I the* ***SON OF MAN*** *am"?*

22

Other examples of Jesus being referred to as the "Son of Man" in the "New Testament" are as follows:

(Matthew 26:2) *"Ye know that after two days is the feast of the Passover, and the **SON OF MAN** is betrayed to be crucified".*

(Matthew 12:40) *"For as Jonas was three days and three nights in the whale's belly; so shall the **SON OF MAN** be three days and three nights in the heart of the earth."*

(John 6:53) *"Ye know that after two days is the feast of the Passover, and the **SON OF MAN** is betrayed to be crucified".*

How can Jesus be both the "Son of God" and the "Son of Man"? Especially, considering that God stated emphatically that he is not a man *(See Numbers 23:19)*. In fact there are easily over sixty (60) passages in the "New Testament" in which Jesus is referred to as the "Son of Man". Yet many still insist that he is the "Son of God".

In short, John's declaration of *"God so loved the world that he gave his **only begotten Son**, that whosoever believeth in him should not perish, but have everlasting life"* is incorrect. The falsehood of this comment is demonstrated in the several references of the multiple "Sons of God". It is further emphasized with David being referred to as God's begotten son. Lastly, this belief is shattered by numerous "New Testament" references to Jesus as the "Son of Man" and Jesus referring to himself as the "Son of Man".

Psalm 146:3 warns us against believing in the "Son of Man". It states, **"Put not your trust in princes, nor in the SON OF MAN, in whom there *is* no help."**

<u>**A Few Additional "New Testament" References of Jesus as the "Son of Man":**</u>

Matthew (16:27), Matthew (17:9), Matthew (17:22), Matthew (20:18), Matthew (20:28), Matthew (25:31), Matthew (26:2), Matthew (26:24), Matthew (26:45), Matthew (26:64), Mark (8:31), Mark (9:9), Mark (10:33), Mark (10:45), Mark (14:21), Mark (14:21), Luke (9:44).

Genealogy

It is evident from the previous chapter that Jesus is not the Son of God, the next logical question is: What is his ancestry, genealogy or lineage? To attempt to answer this question we must review the text of the New Testament. This is necessary because nowhere in the "Old Testament" is there any mention of the name Jesus. Unfortunately, yet expectedly, the New Testament has varying records on the genealogy of Jesus. The varying records of his genealogy are found in Matthew 1:1-16 and Luke 3:23-38.

The first record of Jesus' genealogy is found in Matthew 1:1 –16. Matthew 1: 1 reads, "The book of the genealogy of Jesus Christ the Son of David the Son of Abraham". If Jesus was God's son it would simply read and God begot Jesus through Mary or something similar. Also it is also important to realize that Matthew traced his genealogy to Joseph. If Joseph isn't Jesus father, why would Joseph's genealogy be important? Remember that at the beginning of the chapter it said, "The book of the generation of Jesus Christ". That means that this record is supposed to be just that, the

25

book of the generation of Jesus Christ and his genealogy goes back to Joseph and not to God.

The second version of Jesus genealogy is found in Luke (3:23-38). This alleged genealogy of Jesus goes from Jesus to Adam. Almost immediately you will observe that there are conflicting reports on his ancestry. In Matthew (1:16) it stated that Joseph's fathers name is Jacob. However, as we will see in Luke (3:23) Luke reports that Joseph father name was Heli. There is no accurate record of Joseph's father so how can there be an accurate record of Jesus' ancestry, lineage or genealogy. Some contend that this is Jesus' genealogy in Luke 3 is traced through his mother Mary. To believe this assertion you must believe that without any mention of Mary in the genealogy. Remember that in Luke 3:23 it says "Jesus the son of Joseph the son of Heli the son of Matthat etc" with no mention of Mary anywhere in his genealogy. Also, there is no valid precedent of anyone in the Bible having their genealogy traced through their mother. Lastly, it never stated in Luke 3 that his genealogy was traced through his mother.

26

Let's make the glaring contradictions in Jesus' conflicting genealogy a little clearer. In Matthew 1 and Luke 3 his genealogy is listed in different orders. In Matthew the list ends with Jesus and in Luke it begins with Jesus. This list will be written in the same order which will aid in making the blatant contradictions more obvious. Both lists will conclude with Abraham to save space even though the point is made far before reaching Abraham.

Matthew 1:1-16	Luke 3:23-38
Jesus	Jesus
Joseph	Joseph
Jacob	Heli
Matthan	Matthat
Eliud	Levi
Azor	Melchi
Zerrubabel	Janna
Jeconiah	Joseph
Josiah	Mattathiah
Hezekiah	Amos
Uzziah	Nahum
Jehoshaphat	Esli
Asa	Naggai
Abiah	Maath
Rehoboam	Mattathiah
Solomon	Semei
David	Joseph
Jesse	Judah
Obed	Joannas
Boaz	Rhesa
Salmon	Zerubbabel

Ram
Hezron
Perez
Judah
Jacob
Isaac
Abraham

Shealtiel
Neri
Melchi
Addi
Cosam
Elmodam
Er
Jose
Eliezer
Jorim
Matthat
Levi
Simeon
Judah
Joseph
Jonan
Eliakim
Melea
Menan
Mattathah
Nathan
David
Jesse
Obed
Boaz
Salmon
Nahshon
Amminadab
Ram
Hezron
Perez
Judah
Jacob
Isaac
Abraham

As you can see the two records of Jesus' genealogy are not alike in any manner. The contradictions are evident beginning with the individual stated as being Jesus' grandfather. The writers of the New Testament could not agree on a fact as simple as Jesus' grandfather. This is another indication of the unreliability of the New Testament text and the story of Jesus.

Conclusion

The story of Jesus, especially as found in the New Testament, is highly unreliable. There are far too many contradictions in the stories regarding him as well as inconsistencies to other biblical history and doctrine. The major pillars of the Christian faith are all very flawed in the consistency of the story as well as the ability of the story to be proven. The "virgin" birth story was a misinterpretation of a prophecy; there are multiple conflicting stories on what occurred during Jesus' alleged resurrection. There is tons of evidence that demonstrate that Jesus is not God's only begotten son. Furthermore, Jesus' genealogy is questionable which leads some experts and theologians to question his existence.

The reader is not to assume that the inconsistencies in the story of Jesus and the New Testament prove that the bible as a whole is false. One must recognize that the "New Testament" and the "Old Testament" are separate works of prophecy, history and writings. For example, there was no "New Testament" during the life of Jesus. The "Only Testament" that was around is what is commonly referred

30

to as the "Old Testament". Therefore, anytime Jesus is quoted as commenting on the Laws of God or righteousness his point of reference had to be in the "Only Testament" available. Jesus, if his existence can be verified, never read the "New Testament" because it never existed during his time. Furthermore, there is no mention of the name Jesus in the entire "Old Testament". Additionally, the vast majority of the "Old Testament" was originally written in Hebrew while the "New Testament" was written in Greek. These facts along with a vast list of others demonstrate that the "New Testament" and "Old Testament" are separate theological writings with little or no connection.

.

The main connection of the text is that the "New Testament" verifies the authenticity of the "Old Testament". It is impossible for one to believe in the "New Testament" and not believe in the "Old Testament". Conversely, one can securely believe in and verify the "Old Testament" without accepting the "New Testament" doctrine or accepting Jesus as the messiah. When Jesus is quoted as being asked to declare the greatest commandment in the law, he is quoted as saying, *"Thou shalt love the Lord thy God with all thy heart, and*

31

with all thy soul, and with all thy mind." (Matthew 22: 36 – 37). This is a quote from the "Old Testament" *(Deuteronomy 6:5).* If you believe in Jesus' doctrine then you must believe in the "Old Testament" because he did. With the "Old Testament" being the only verifiable testament it can be righteously, logically and spiritually concluded that the "Old Testament" is the "Only Testament" of the Most High God. Furthermore, if you still believe in the validity of Jesus upon the completion of reading this text you must consider that the Only Testament that he would have followed during his life time is the one referred to as the "Old Testament'.

Notes:

Notes:

www.ingramcontent.com/pod-product-compliance
Lightning Source LLC
La Vergne TN
LVHW051713080426
835511LV00017B/2896